"Happy Birthday
Datina
2011

Hope you enjoy this
book of poetry. Wishing
you the best....
                    Corie ♡

Blue Abundance

Blue Abundance

NOËL HANLON

salmonpoetry

Published in 2010 by
Salmon Poetry
Cliffs of Moher, County Clare, Ireland
Website: www.salmonpoetry.com
Email: info@salmonpoetry.com

ISBN 978-1-907056-47-5

Cover image: *from "Signs of Life" (2003), a photographic series by Kristy Edmunds,*
originally exhibited at the Elizabeth Leach Gallery, Portland, Oregon, USA.
Reproduced with the kind permission of the artist.
Cover design & typesetting: *Siobhán Hutson*
Printed in England by imprint*digital*.net

In memory of

JOHN O'DONOHUE
(1956 – 2008)

who dreamed of this book for me while alive
and is seeing it through with eternal eyes.

Acknowledgements

Grateful Acknowledgment is made to the editors of the following publications in which earlier versions of some of these poems first appeared: *The Texas Observer* and *Poetry Ireland Review*.

Huge gratitude to the following people who made this book possible: to Jessie and Siobhán at Salmon Poetry; to my sister (the first poet I ever knew), Gail Hanlon, and Catherine Johnson for their inspirational readings of my manuscript; to Naomi Shihab Nye and Judith Barrington for believing in my poems; to my poetry group: Ursula, Bette, Caroline, Molly, Kari, Barbara and Jeannette for all the fun and brilliant hours of critique; to the O'Donohues, for the laughter, love and generosity of family when I'm in Ireland; to Kristy Edmunds for her loving focus on the cover of this book; and to Peter, Maura and Paul for their very necessary love, encouragement and for unselfishly giving me the time to write.

Contents

III. The Earth Loves Her Body

IV. Familiar Mystery

I. The View From Here Tells Us Everything

Beneath Reflection

for Bess

Sometimes the river opens
her pure reflection of landscape
where trees lean in and discover
their slenderness tenderly painted.
Once in awhile, a messenger, say
a salmon, rinsed pink
as sunrise, breaks the surface,
like laughter in church
reminds us, we only know
this side of what we see.

In Mexico, our eyes were willing
the salty distance into becoming
a beach we could land on when
the gray whale slid up inside
the deeper gray swirl of waves.
Our blue boat tipped sideways as
each body inside reached out to touch
what had always swam beyond us.

Returning to a lake, religiously
each summer, to dive naked into
the clear solitude of its sides, to open
my eyes where the otters swim beneath
fallen cedars and skim the silted stones,
I may have thought I knew it inside out.
But once, when the moon was a generous path,
I slipped a kayak in and lay back inside
shadows of mountains that hold everything in.
Then, the stillness began to bump against
the thin shell that held me separate.
All around the sliver of my boat,
the blackness stirred and sucked.
Fish were kissing the night and I
was terrified and certain.

Now I will borrow
a boat or walk the slick banks
of dawn when earth's breath
is rising into cold starlight
and there is no division between
water and sky. Adrift, as if existence
is no more difficult than the patient wading
of a great blue heron. Something unexpected
will slice the world I believed
I knew before in two.

Peaches

1.

We wanted to pick peaches,
but packing them is what girls did
in that one-café town
under ocher palisades
that silently pried colors
of the violent sun down
one by one. Nights we slept
with our heads to the cliff
faces, in orchards beneath,
kept our clothes and books
in peach crates, and washed
our blood-stained underwear
in a murky stretch
of the Colorado River.
The black stone wall behind us
confirmed sheets of lusty stars,
ephemeral dials of moonlight
drifted across our breasts.

2.

A wall of daylight lit the open air shed
where we stood alongside the blurred arms
of other women and culled the bruised peaches,
rolling by us like little heads.
When I saw the men in need of a hand
I stepped out of line. Once
I loaded boxes into trucks
with two brothers who spoke
Spanish. Our silence, our sweat,
slid between us, as they worked faster
because I was there, and I worked as fast

to prove that I could, until
the oldest one grabbed me,
squeezed my arms so they hurt,
kissed me with a passionate tongue,
let go and went back to work
so quickly it was hard to conceive
how it happened at all.

3.

We ate peaches warm from the trees,
soft fur we broke with the bared teeth
of youth. Sweet thick water soothed
our thirst and seared in memory
the first taste away from home.

The pruned trees gave the shade
of parents, the brilliant leaves like eyes,
sheltered us, until mornings grew crisp
and we lifted our heads to a new range
of mountains and crawled up the red canyons
into the burnt clattering hills of aspen.

Second Chance

In anger, my mother dragged her children
down rivers formed long before them.
On the dark trails she charged along,
the deep green sway of gods
and the large quiet family
I knew were there, were lost on her.

I bring home heavy round stones,
who keep the silence of mountains.
In corners, on ledges, they hold
the warm flat hand of the sun.

Until my children pushed through me
and I heard the hunger of separation,
until they brought their wild grassy heads
and leaned deeply into my breast,
I had forgotten: we are born
expecting everything.

They don't follow me to the edge
of our land where blue heron lift
heavily from the shallow, where
a fat gleaming beaver slides quietly
into the skin of the creek, leaving
a soft ringing wake. To hear me tell them
it is true is enough for now.

They want more from the world
than it may ever give them.
They open that part of me.

In Your Life

Whatever else is true or right in this life, there remains
a steady pattern – falling oval sunlight and floundering shadows.
When the light is touching you some other half is in darkness.
However, do not bring this up casually at a candlelit dinner party.
Cars can take you over the rough-tooth mountains, into pure blue sky,
but you'll come home again.
Months will pass when you never take those soft, sinking steps,
leading you into earth – and earth doesn't care
whether you do or do not –
but the minute you drop the handle of whatever burden you carry
and wander off, you enter a place in your life
that was meant to be huge.
Still, your mind won't leave you alone;
you're already collecting yourself to drive the children home,
writing a list of other things to pick up in order to save time.
But then a shadow lifts from the corners, an incremental shift
which pulls you out of the crowded rooms.
Maybe you're merely closer to your death but you feel
as if you are only now just arriving in your life.
The moment you leave the house, walk through the gate
toward that wild promise,
you're making a path through a dark stand of evergreens,
to the clearing only you can see.

As It Is

Beneath us, a maze of tunnels;
you have to be patient to watch
the quivering vegetables before
they're tugged under and devoured.

And above, intelligent eyes perch,
observe us until we leave, then swoop
down to pull up the tear shaped kernels
when their first leaves emerge.

Around us, our mountains
have become illusive, weightless;
their solid, blue bases melting
in the haze of pollution.

Inside, a stack of books grows,
opened to the underlined wisdoms
of those who live to work in gardens,
reaping alongside that which is lost.

Imprint

When I upend the heavy coverings
on the two dry wells and peer down
in awe of the unknown artist
whose mind conceived the beautiful
cylindrical depths, whose hands
lined the walls with bricks so perfectly
they've never caved in to earth,
enduring longer than the water
table they drew from here,
it is only the surface I've disturbed
that clatters to utter quiet.

But the house has an echo of its own
we've grown into. Alone,
I hear a memory in the grain
of the old-growth wood when the worn
floorboards crack and groan under
the weight of invisible footsteps – perhaps
hers, who first polished them when
she filled these rooms with children,
who lived through the Depression
when wheat was planted up to the walls,
erasing a path to the front porch.

She was either feared or loved;
her life was flowerless and hard.
When she died she took the key
to the front door with her
and we, like her aged daughters,
cannot pass through it unless
it's opened from inside.

Exile

He craves the bitter greens
his wife plants for him
but cannot trust himself
to pick anything, terrified
he'll mistake them
for something poisonous.

On summer evenings, in Oregon,
he follows his son outside into
their strip of garden, on the edge
of a city forest, determined never to
show his fear, even as his son thrusts
his hand into briars and gathers
a fistful of blackberries. But when
the plump, stained fingers open
toward him, offering, he cannot
bring himself to eat from them.

Raised by parents who escaped
death in Nazi camps,
who refused to eat anything
that wasn't wrapped in cellophane,
what could the earth have hoped
to teach him, cemented beneath
the weight of New York City?

An Air About Her

My mother calls me
and her voice triggers
dead electrical wire
running behind old,
rough walls.

Immediately my shoulders are locked
in rooms of houses we sold,

but the hinges are old,
they let me out
to breathe fresh air.

She calls me and her voice
tampers with the paper-thin
air between us. She pulls out
the scissors that were never put back
in the same drawer.

My phones are always by windows,
my eyes outside. I remind myself
our views are thousands of miles apart.

Mother's Day

What did you do with your day?
Not a thing. I slept in this chair,
I had a dream in the afternoon.

What was your dream?
I was in our house calling and calling your father,
who wouldn't answer. I was so angry!

Which house were you in?
The huge one, just outside
of Boston.

What was life like for you then?
I can't remember
for the life of me.

I remember you left us for Europe then.
You don't say.
Well I'll be.

So, you were angry because he wouldn't answer?
Yes, I called and called
but he never came.

Well, you know he is dead.
Hah!
I guess that's right.

Do you ever miss him?
No,
he was always a burden to me.

Yet you were calling him to you?
Yes,
now you tell me what that was about!

South of the Border

Where Mexico's hourglass
grows thin, pouring south,
the sand is coarse, crushed shells.

Days singed by fierce light
peel off all coats of dullness,
embroider whites with fiery color.

Woven beneath fans of palm
the deepest shade pools
like water held in dark blue tiles.

We are foreigners for a while
floating as if weightless,
lulled by a romance language.

Dawn breaks cadmium red there
where birds like flowers unfurl
white wings from emerald branches.

Our dreams envy the morning
we woke and boated a rich lagoon
before flying home into sheets of ice.

Vertigo

Beneath the gray spinning of high-pressure systems, morning tosses
    away the key.
Inside her, the smell of winter's decay rises and follows her where
    she breathes.

Keeping herself carefully still, she secretly folds and puts away her truer
self, like her mother's silk scarves, never worn, anticipating a future.

On days like these she resolves not to move her person,
though thoughts like visitors come and go freely from that prison.

She can view the weight and warp of gravity in old glass, but cannot
see through to the mountain whose liquid core swirls up, reforms
    what blew off.

She dreams of an island; in certain light it appears to grow nearer,
(a sign to the mainlanders that bad weather's arrival should be feared).

The floor will not move as light whirls and slides across its surfaces.
Hours upon hours fall like a ringing phone, a prankster no one traces.

Soon, the afternoon's door will open and her son will pour in.
He may or may not notice that nothing has changed but him.

Later still, in vernal darkness, her husband will return again,
empty handed, his sinking heart whorls downward as it drains.

It seems impossible for her to change the scene in front of her eyes.
If she moves, even slightly, the truth may spill up from her inside.

"August Night"

for the painter, Anne Appleby

Canvas of penetrable midnight blue,
its source of light's reflection visible.
Painted when the artist's heart was new,
on the cusp of embarking, visceral.
The fabric of darkness opens
and we're set afloat in an ocean.

A boat sailing in the ether,
tethered only by a red thread.
We circle inside the infinite, teeter
among shapes, ancestral presences.
We're cast through a sweeping net
of gentle light and color's essences.

Neither falling nor rising but held in
the brush of the creator, the unseen
sings to us, lures us toward
a lit threshold fathoms within.
There the heart breaks forward,
imagines a choice between
passion and peace.

Faux Village

While U.S. bombs annihilated an eighth century city in Iraq,
The Given Garden, a village was made here in Oregon, sprang up
from a gutted-for-gravel-field I'd passed by for years on our freeway.
No one will ever live there yet everyday its parking-lot fills and empties
with consumer hunger. Out of my element, I've made the pilgrimage,
because it's convenient and spring has made me green with envy,
the way it swirls in wild colors, and in contrast: everything I own
is washed out or black. Unfortunately, I mistakenly begin my search
in the petites, deflated when I eventually find myself/my size
in the XL section. Racks of florals, lace, frills, empress waists,
flattering tucks and feminine folds to choose from.
Perhaps you'd prefer instead a powder blue to go with the grey pants?
suggests the friendliest-in-America clerk, casually hovering around me.
But I begin to suffocate as her eyes drop to where my waistline
should be, to my hemline – *so not Capri* – however, my shoes
are curiously stylish, but that's when I walk out. In the street,
untroubled parents clutch coffee, lounge in sunlight beside gleeful
children splashing in a shallow water feature. Piped-out
Neil Young songs follow me everywhere I walk; it's over-the-top
too nice, so I duck into a store whose signage reveals nothing
about what treasures my life exists without. I meander through aisles
of stuff while the meek, smiling cashier begs me to ask her
any questions I've got … I'm tempted but temper myself,
do not indulge my humor or doubts. I wander until I come to a dead-end
and find hanging there, dangling in four foot, glittering letters,
the word WISH. *Well, that's nice, but maybe not.*
What would they hope I might wish? For an item which could never fit
in my rough kitchen? For peace? I wished then, more than anything,
that I'd known Baghdad before the U.S. dropped in.

Gravel Shoulder

Down the road
which neither rises
nor falls, but runs hard
due south until sweat pours
sweetly from my brow
and I begin to believe my legs
will carry me as far as my heart
desires, just where the road takes a turn
westward, swerves to avoid an old stand
of trees, whose wide reaching branches
defy gravity or define strength
in balance, or both, I found
a migratory bird lying still
on the pavement. Stopping,
I saw its breast was cleanly slit
open, a tiny heart poured out.
When I carried the small body
safely to the roots of the oaks,
I felt her still supple and inside
her eye, not yet hazed-over,
I imagined I could see the flight
which killed her only moments ago.
Nearby, killdeers cried their two-syllable
alarm, dragged their wings behind them,
as if broken, to lure me away from nests
they have built into the shifting gravel
shoulder of the road I was on.

My Daughter's Window

While you were gone I came into your room
and heard a desperate thrumming, coming
from inside your diaphanous, purple curtains.
It was a hummingbird, pinned between
two panes of glass in your open window.
One wing caught upwards, the other furiously
beating. My heart sped to her though I froze
terrified that in trying to free her I'd break
her tiny wings. Yet once I began to weave
my hands beneath her she stilled until
I aimed her at open space and she vanished
as an arrow freed in the green wilderness.

Each May in Co. Clare

For years, always in the far-off, she calls
from the cleaved and washed-dark hills, and I've listened.
I've swept clean the barren distance, searching

through the glow of white buds on blackthorns
for any quivering. As I sit in stillness, on the cold level
pavement leading to an abandoned village,

the distinctness of her song has become
inseparable from my experience of green
birthing; spring after winter's famine

in a limestone wilderness where blue gentians,
buttery primrose, and lavender or rarer-white orchids
stand beside stinging nettles, thriving on plates of stone.

When she suddenly settles like the Atlantic wind
on the other side of the wall I'm leaning against,
I shift as fluently as the cattle grazing

to catch a glimpse of her just as she dips away
from a branch. And having named her by her call
I smile as I call back, cuckoo! Farewell!

Climbing Above Hell Roaring Creek

for Peter

Ascending the red pumice mountain,
as if drawn to the most difficult
to reach, we leave the effortless meadows
of mariposa lilies and quenching springs,
go further, where there are no trails,
but faded flags, only I seem to see,
waving from the sparse arms of trees.
You call me when you lose sight of me.

The mountain turns my name
around in its hard mouth and swallows.
You follow me through the opening
into the red bowl of a sleeping volcano.
We share the precious last drops of water,
where no one could stay longer than moments,
though the view from here tells us everything
about beginnings and exposed betweens.

Our breathing twines in the final effort,
carries us back to the oval body
of water where I strip and swim across
while you carry my clothes and walk around
the lip of the lake edged with reeds that bend
from the weight of blue, mating dragonflies.
We meet on the other side where we have tied
our single kayak, where we share a fire.

On The Shoreline

To taste the ocean is like tasting one's
own blood; a ritual that has become
the way I enter the immensity,
before walking beside divinity.
An hour alone along the weaving forms
can clear the sullen heart between its storms,
can rinse, as music does, the sullied thoughts
– their chords of tangled and monotonous
chorus – until each voice inside comes clean.
The cadenced waves reset the way we breathe.

After the storm, the washed sands are engraved;
calligraphy of kelp the sea has made
here, where our footprints vanish in the tides
to show us how impermanent our lives.

At last the wind has stilled on All Soul's Eve
and from a cliff I look down on the sea,
loosed after drinking spirits with a friend,
who said good-night not knowing I'd descend
the steep lawn to sit alone in moonlight.
The moon is full, the ocean at high tide,
so hushed and fully lit like a liquid pearl,
it makes me feel that I have caught the world
in its most intimate moment, as if God
is here and I can sense how I am not.

Hidden Port

(Puerto Escondito)

When I woke in the foreign night
before the music had stopped,
the shapes of shadows so unlike
what falls across my walls at home,
I was content to slip beneath
the open windows and listen
to the drifting rafts of other lives.
Men were singing somewhere
out where boats are dragged up
onto sand each night. The soft crush
of waves and a distant drumming,
then a rooster before silence took
the night a little deeper, before
a thread of light unraveled the dawn
and pulled apart the locked iron gates
for those who would rise soon to work.
In those hours, I went a long way inward,
inside a language where I cannot remain,
with its passive verbs and no future tense.

Barn Owl

for Pat

When you unlocked the door
to your barn in France, our shadows
and a slat of brightness fell in,
slashing the darkness that had been
sealed inside for months.
Together, we stepped in.

While our eyes expanded,
the embedded cobbles
in the ancient walls
and the hand-hewn beams
above us shyly came forward.

Then a soft clapping higher up,
further than our eyes were ready
to perceive, but it seemed
to carry its own source of light
in piercing white wings.

So strikingly close
when I close my eyes, it continues
to hunt for us through the dark,
like a blessing for wisdom
between us and the unseen.

Between Two Blue Abstracts

If God was never beaten into you but grew
naturally instead, between two blue abstracts
of Sorrow and Birth, you would have gazed
with the openness of an infant
at the breast of a depressed mother
and taken it all in.

You would be unafraid of sadness in others,
recognize it as common, how it dwells in eyes
and in wilderness where springs well up, weeping
faces of stone walls where trees hang on
against all odds.

You'd hear loneliness in a ping, echoing
of a raven caw, a stone dropped into a hollow place,
wings like knives cutting the blue silence.

You'd find delight in the heavy ringing
of steeple bells, but lose count of the marked hours,
always somewhere between sleep and rising.
Praying could feel like mere daydreaming.

Sermons couldn't adhere to you,
they'd separate or join like mercury drops
loosed from broken thermometers.
After a while only poetry would make sense.

In any given moment you'd know birth
is present, opposite sorrow, possible
and possibly God, laughter, or anything
expanding light from a dark blue core.

Winter's Scripture

for John O'Donohue

Each view reinvents itself
with dawn, a gradual blue engages gray.
Some days the fog prevents a distance
needed for definition. Dreams jam up
with daylight, the plum barn looms close
to the house, as if morning ends there.

Today the red veins of what's still alive
come forward through the dead gold.
Each strand of the hazel wood catkins
hangs like a tidy thought, their yellow-
green is the underworld of fields.

The earth loves her body,
even in this season where sadness washes
over and through her. Owl hoots soften
the nights, lift them to tree branches.
Geese gently bend the silence that lives
beneath everything we do.

The spindly trees we planted along our border
lean in the direction of winter storms.
They know what we dream for them
but lose hope in the news of the wind.
Perrett Mountain lifts itself
out of the river's blanket, gets on
with its day, its horse fields and tree farms.
But the valley stays folded inside fog.

Today I lit candles before dawn
to pray the light into view. It seemed
to help me. Like the land
standing under water.
There is nothing to do but reflect,
nowhere more present than here.

II. This Slant of Harvest

This Slant of Harvest

From the dining-room window I watch you herd
the lambs into the cage of the truck. Autumn's
weakening light leans hard on the afternoon.
A stacked shadow of the barn, full of oats and straw,
falls across the bleached stubble of our field.
Suddenly all we coaxed to life in spring
weighs on us with what must be harvested.
The purple plums, stolen from drunken yellow-jackets,
split open in our hands. The green tomatoes, staked
in June, become burdens to their own vines, ripen
all at once in September's dry nights. We simmer them
in their juices until they float like summer lanterns
in jars lining the shelves of a dark cellar.
We'll preserve the sweet, alter the sour,
plunder the garden before winter ploughs it under.
Everything feels tinged with the sting and prickle of loving.

Elegy for My Father

What you do not have you find everywhere.
W.S. Merwin

As long as you lived there was comfort
on the other end of the line, a buffer between
your children and our mother's dark garden.

When the drought broke, the sunflowers
whose roots grew too close to the surface
toppled over. One downpour erased summer
from the air, filled it with hard memory
instead, with slow death.

It was autumn when I knew I would lose you,
when the scent of illness rose in your rooms.
And in winter I was ready to let you go,
the body I loved my entire life, thoroughly
ruined. It was with love that I released you.

Twenty autumns. Once again, I am harvesting
the garden, freezing what will help me remember
warmth, preparing myself for winter's dearth of it.
My son, who carries your name, your humor,
and my daughter, at my breast while you died,
now live far from home.

When they lowered the pine box, holding your form,
into the new year's frozen ground, you weren't there,
you were becoming the fearless presence behind me,
here, even now, in these words, in these seasons.

Flower

for Illo

The flower is brilliant, it is not afraid
to lose its petals, its sex, its meetings
with bees. It wants to go to seed.
Small quick birds carry this
message in their beaks.

Annie

The ewe whose life I tried to save
last spring, who died and was stripped clean
in one week of summer's heat by vultures,
is now scattered in the grass where her sisters graze.
Only the sturdy backbone and stubborn skull
recall her name.

At Equinox

Autumnal light hoards
its colors inside the skin of squash,
our appetites deepen, everything inward.

There is a solemnity just beneath
our light-hearted feasts of lamb
dinners, in the weeks after slaughter.

The swallows who spent summer
weaving the warp and weft of nest
are really married to air,
abandon us too swiftly.

The light falls distracted, thinner,
searching the earth for solitude,
while we stubbornly stand out
culling any remnants.

Headlights

At that hour before fall
when the sun just rounds down,
the world is dim with signs
of life invisible; deer are hit,
crossing over is possible.

We were laughing and crying
at the same time, our father's body still
on his bed and my baby was waving
up, up where she may have seen his spirit
sifting, but ours were weighted down
by the gravity of separation.

In the eight years since,
my hair has gone white,
as if my own darkness were lifting
into the blurred ceiling of earth,
readying me for a cradle of air.

I always see the deer just in time,
stunned shadows with the round, wet eyes
of a god, unblinking inside the blinding
white of my headlights, before I skid
and they leap from my sight.

Serious Rain

A serious rain arrives on the dying fields
dousing the embers of drying leaves, raising
a new chilling mist in the near distance
that takes the din of human industry deep
into the drumbeat of Autumn, making
what we love hard to love: my mother fading
away into a time when hours mean nothing,
my garden's tender heart riddled with slugs,
my dogs, carrying the oil of poison oak on their coats.
Autumn always chants like this.
Why do we fool ourselves thinking we could be separate
creatures from nature's irrefutable desire?

The East Wind

There is little goodness
in this unrelenting wind
which ushers in winter,
though it opens the gray tomb
of uncertain light to a blue,
where a moon that's been missing
is strung low on the horizon,

where a distant sun licks
the wounds of frost. What will
survive must draw downward
the brittle remains of old growth
to nourish dormant roots beneath.

Listening to the keening
through interminable nights,
I become almost immune to its complaint,
though I sense that it carries
others' suffering: lost children, famine
on its desperate wings.

I wake in the eye of its sudden quiet,
thinking how like giving birth
this moment is, when labor halts,
while the shoulders of the unborn
turn before the unbearable pushing
can begin again.

January 4, 2009

The only light that night
was my friend's inspiration
to leave the house –
after kissing his children –
and climb the mountain,
walk through its darkness
over broken stone
and deep crevices,
to the wide hole
at the heart of it
to light a memorial fire
for his brother.

The only warmth
was his sister's hand
in mine and the whiskey
we carried until

we reached the rim
and looked down to find
him shining in firelight,
like a bright planet reflecting
in an inverted universe
we've become intimate with.

Too Soon

In memory of John O'Donohue

Stand still and do not waver from your emptiness;
for at this time you can turn away, never to turn back again.
Meister Eckhart

In the bleak dream that is February's,
I will myself to face this wilderness
I've inherited by your leaving us,
hoping to still find something of you here.

Inside the grey hills of sky, a heaving,
and in the emptying of breath, a thrill,
leaning as I am, with all my senses,
toward a nothingness that calls you nearer.

But spring begins to till the dark I need
for grieving my loss with a thoroughness.
And through the chill of distance: moss, lichen,
the budded reaching of red branch, assume

colors and light you loved. The living world
reaches for me, bereaved of you, too soon.

Bittersweet

Timidly faithful to light, as the heart is,
cottonwood buds begin opening, slowly
glowing like a candle lit before darkness
brightens it. Coppery-green or a viridine-
yellow, resinous leaves, yet unfolded, release
their fragrance on wind; it is amber honey,
a memory – tasting the colors of flowers.
The first fork of the food that you lift
to your mouth after learning
someone you love has just died.

Beauty Visits, Never Stays

for Mares

The last time, just after
we opened his coffin
to let him say good-bye
to the presence of the house
he loved and felt loved by,
then followed him back
as a majestic rainbow like a gate
to the eternal, arched over us
as we left Conamara
on his last journey
down to his birthplace.

> *Each person's rainbow, like his or her reflection in a pool of water,*
> *is uniquely determined by the point where he or she stands,*
> *by the angle between eye, raindrop, and sun.*

Here alone, now, I know surely
as the violet-blue bruised sky
between double-rainbows, lingering
too long to be ephemeral, he is
where he always said we'll be:
"no where"," behind the house", closer
to us than the solid stone outside, holding
my eye, a flitting bird.

To arrive here, I had to look through
my heart, with a certain angle of radiant
thought, and my tears.

(Italicized words, including the title are from *Wonder, The Rainbow and the Aesthetics of Rare Experience*, by Philip Fisher)

The Red Wing

The beauty of the song
of the red wing blackbird
is enough and not for long.

The brilliance of the migrating
bird song was given,
changed nothing but the moment
it captured the garden,
the imagination, the dispirit heart
and moved on to stay alive.

III. The Earth Loves Her Body

Farmer

for P.J.

The garden he tills each spring
Is where it has always been
He can see his father there
Praying while he weeded

He reads stories
Everywhere on his land
The unmarked graves
Of the unbaptized children
And the nameless traveler

Where his uncle planted
A tree or built a wall or cairn
Where he buried his favorite dog

Where he stood as a young man
When his brother asked him
What he was thinking
As they weeded the turnips
Which he hated
Which was his answer

The trees he will never cut
Swayed by a memory of laughter

He knows where
The badgers nest
The springs rise
Where there's shelter
If he's caught out
In a rain-shower
Where the stone holds
Ancient ocean forms
Where it sings
With streams beneath

Like the auburn fox
That he feeds outside the kitchen
He moves across his land
Gracefully and exposed
He never asked for it
It was given to him

The Conamara Farmer

Carrying a torn canvas sack
full of turf along the boreen
between the shed and house
I come against the neighbor
and he calls out to me
You fit in around here alright!
which I gladly take to heart
invite him in and put on the tea
as he sinks into a seat by the fire
in his wellies and winter coat
to talk about the price of oil
and how the government
has got into his fields
how he wishes they never got in
at all as farmers were better off
before, not expecting much
as long as there was a little
something on the table.
He liked the old ways.
Electricity fecked everything up
because you could see everything
at night before there were lights.
And he wonders about death
how if you could weigh life
wouldn't it be heavier
with sorrow than happiness?
which leads him to something
that continues to bother him –
do you think it is possible to be happy
and not know it?

Strength

Some days I carry my farm like a burden.
A longing, as unavoidable as death,
sweeps away what I hadn't known
was peace until then, and I walk
a wide circle around my happiness,
study gravity, fallen branches,
the bowed fence-line.

I've learned on days like these
to move into my fields on peasant feet,
to reach for the long rope of muscle
running the length of arm and spine,
to heave the work that needs to be done.

I open the door to the pen where
I have kept the lame ram, cut away
the rotted hoof until blood runs
and I'm sure I've reached living tissue.
Released, he limps into light,
raises his head to the scent of green.

And I bend, follow white threads,
tenacious roots of morning glory,
until my soil appears to gleam
and I overhear a conversation
full of seedlings, uncurling
inside their dark home.

When night sifts back in I know
I could flick on false streams,
could sort through all that has come
undone, but I don't. I open
windows and let motes of dust,
like ghosts, drift out.

I find my hands, best friends,
stained and cracked with love
of earth, at rest, at last.
I trust in the ancient walls that define
my life and the infinite darkness
falling into sight.

Kate's Twin

While I slept, pulling the warmth of my husband's body into my own,
a black lamb was being born, dropped onto a floor of matted straw.

Inside the clear unbroken sack, he must have raised his head
in expectation before suffocating on his first breath,

his twin already unfolded, flinging herself toward the scent of sustenance.
I woke to the voices of coyotes and the north wind overlapping.

He was still in a shroud of steam when I lifted his slippery form
into the frozen world, certain I could see a heart beat.

In uncolored daylight I took down a shovel from summer's hook
and scraped a small hole out of difficult earth, folded his legs to fit him in.

I scattered the sweet oats that would have set
his mother's milk for twins over the scalped ground.

I do not know what animals feel, but pilgrim eyes yearned
toward my fields today. Translucent hooves never scratched the earth.

His sister thrives, I give her a name. Already miniscule flowers of the filberts
scent the air, and delicate blades of oat grass green over the grave.

Spring Lambs

(after "Winter Lambs", by Jane Kenyon)

Only a fortnight ago, the air
remembered Easter mornings
when we rose before children
to hide boiled, blood-red eggs.
But an Arctic wind came in,
so we covered the fooled shoots
of spring with straw and blankets,

and nervously eyed the ewes'
wide bellies. Lambs imminent,
judging their readiness by
the heaviness of their bags,
the pinkness of their vulvas,
for if lambs dropped in this wind,
in moments of our negligence,

it would mean a culpable death.
The friend I depend on, who doesn't hesitate
to pull the lamb that comes too slowly or to shove
into submission the ewe who won't feed her lamb,
was listening to her mother's last breaths,

while I stretched my arm
up into the uterus of a yearling,
grabbed the legs of her lamb
whose head was stuck, pulled
with everything I had. It was like watching
someone giving birth, she said later,

about her mother's dying.
Between the moments of our own first
and last breath, we are doubtful participants,
wondering where we belong.
And like spring on the brink
of winter, we root for life.

Manual Labor

In spring, my hands
gripping the handle
of a spade each day
to soften the earth,
are growing numb.

As I work, I think
of it as a form
of prayer, feeding
some, saving no one.

Deciduous

Leaves take their time
gather the air
nod agreement
with the sky
the way children
ready to be born
give invisible signals
even doctors cannot predict
and the stem breaks

We say this is their last dance
as they slide and spin
to the ground
but secretly I think
they feel their trees
through pores of earth
soft with remains
feel themselves
gathered by roots
becoming memory
in veins of darkness
drawn up through
rings of years
blindly pushed through
branch twig bud
each sheath tighter
more tender
until they explode
in soft green bodies
of spring

Milling About

The old rooster, having proclaimed
too many times, long before and after
dawn, *the sun has risen*, switches
to his other job on earth, to tell
the hens when he's found remnants
of green in the scratched-brown coop-yard.
And they, with their useless wings lifted,
race to him with their hunger, answering,
I'm coming! I'm hungry! The young rooster,
holds back, he knows to test his tiny, red-crowned-glory
in the shadows of the coop, his tenuous crowing
where the old rooster is not. And the Aracanas,
wilder, like grounded hawks, are silent,
do not mingle with the hybrids
– the Red Sex Links or the black and white
Lacewings – they choose the quiet instead,
find the furthest corners of the coop to hide
their jewels, their delicate blue-green eggs,
while the brown and white layers squabble
over who shall get the best (warmest?) boxes
to lay in. Indignant ruckuses erupt, someone
has pushed someone out of a broody nest,
someone is being hen-pecked, insulted or assaulted.
All the while, the kind old rooster, continues
searching for scraps, muttering promises,
with such undying hopefulness and devoted focus
that the hens continue to mill around him.
And then it will happen, with some unseen tilt
of hours in his eye, he cries out, *daylight's going!*
One by one then they straggle back in the coop,
long before night, as if sunlight makes sound
safe. While it drops, they gather into a silence.
Except for the thump of talons clamping on
roost-beams, or the whoosh of settling,
domesticated wings, there is only the murmuring –
as close as chickens ever come to singing –
of peace.

In Oregon

In a lush ravine
between clear-cut
and slashed mountains,
deciduous trees gather in
the August honey light
with the ravenous hunger
of a bear ambling closer
to winter. Shriveled
by drought, a creek
diverts itself to one
side of its wilder form,
hugs the concaved
banks it carved out
with spring's run-off,
in shade, stays luminous.
Everything holds in
its braided song
when the logging
trucks grind
down gears,
roaring against corners
and the time it takes
to grow the majestic.

The softest sounds
then trickle back
into the wake of silence,
like a ripple
illuminates stillness
or the halo
reveals the darkest
shape of shadow.

Trillium

When the fingers of change
were just about to move me away
from the wild places I knew by heart,
I picked the white and red veined
trillium until my hands were filled.
I ran along the muddy thrust of path
while the back of my mind sang
the warning, "they only appear
every seven years" to sleep. I reached
the concrete, where black tar filled
the cracks of my street, held it
together in an intricate puzzle.

Dusk brought fathers home.
My mother at the stove,
her neck hard with feelings,
received the clean stars
and smiled, filled a jar
with water to quench
their emerald stem's thirst,
as urgent as mine.
I would have believed her smile
could lighten our lives, that I
could place in her heart, as easily
as she placed the trillium on the dinner table,
the simple musk of the path that had led me home.

Narcissus

In the end
I will be as the spring flower
the mystery being this:
held in the bulb beneath,
finding the clearest water
without thirst, love
without another,
and my words
only echo
only echo
and my words
without another,
without thirst, love
finding the clearest water
held in the bulb beneath,
the mystery having been this:
I will be as the spring flower
in the end.

Earth's Lace

We could not bring ourselves
to destroy the old webs;
the fragile, white cloth
caught on the black oak
beams in the kitchen,
though the spider itself
was large enough to tear us
away from our tête-à-tête,
so we trapped it in a glass,
freed it in the courtyard,
imagining a silent return
through the cracks after
witnessing its persistence
in spinning panels of light.

Turning to the plowed field,
bending down to look through
the low afternoon sun,
we saw for the first time —
though it was surely there
every autumn — thousands
of white threads, strung from dark
clod to dark clod; the weaving
of an iridescent veil, stretched
across what we'd thought
was fallow before
those illumined moments
when the delicate
lace of our shared world
was made perceptible.

Laugh Lines

The trees are reading
the wild lines of the wind,
whatever it is telling them
is filled with happy light.
They bend just as we do
when laughter runs
through our limbs.

Three Aspens of Tumalo

Already, in August, they shift
currencies, sensing before we do
a brittleness to the nights.
They turn to gold, dappling
brightness into their own shadows.

By moonlight, they seem unblemished
– apparitions – but in daylight
the white pages of bark are inscribed
with blackened lines of old wounds.
Where limbs have been sawed off
dark eye shapes look back at us.

An altar of scarred pillars,
whose crowns touch to create
a living green cathedral.

If one stirs in its own stream
the others listen; the pause between
the final note of wind and the applause
of leaves. The wind enters them,
they're easily swayed
and full of willingness.

Water diviners, their speech is love
of rain, streams, secret rivers
beneath the dusty ground.
They send their roots ahead
of them – their saplings
spring from there.

They'll hold their breath all winter,
silenced, waiting for snow
to melt into their pulse. For now
they still shimmer like children
in playgrounds of wind.

The Gardener

for Alice

Amending the soil for years,
continually pulling the weeds
that reappear, distinguishing them
from flowers, learning
how often to water and fertilize
is an art earned
over years of devotion.

The day arrives
when she turns it over
and effortlessly it unfolds
ready to be seeded.
She realizes the earth
she's worked reveals itself
to her. All she has planted
comes back to her
in unplanned abundance.

IV. Familiar Mystery

Old Kiss

I dreamt a poet's kiss,
our tongues fused, became one
lick of fire. And then I woke
to February's cold room,
your flannel chest just
where my head expects its pillow.
I'll admit I held onto that dream,
sank back into its weft of heat.

When we married we
warmed the bare rooms, spread
over each other. Tables and chairs
accumulated around our comfort, my body
swelled. We loved that tight deep drum
of love sounding in me. Our babies
settled us. A crib and high-chair appeared
and their green eyes – of another world –
stared into our bed, drooled over
our skin, turned to our voices.

Our lovemaking, hushed
and careful not to wake anyone,
learned how to slow and be thankful,
as the hurry to the fire vanished
with the firm contours of my body.
We sit now around that fire
cooking dinner for our children.

We kiss
and our tongues tell on us.
We are hurried or tired or wanting
to curl up. I want those blind kisses
that fused us for life. They were flushed
with the feeling of color. They are hard
to put words to. I grow warm remembering
the touch of their hunger on me.

Relinquishing Time

Waiting at the gate to your summer,
the air was sweet with thrush and hemlock.
We looked into our same green eyes
smiling and gazed away, into
the darker green understory.

I believed while I carried you
in me you'd arrive a girl,
so when I held a boy I was surprised —
never dreaming you could come
to be so like me.

One night last winter, I watched you
drive off — a little too fast
for comfort — red taillight's beacon,
diminished by the distance,
speeding across the black horizon line.

Above you a full moon rose,
partially eclipsed. Rare moments
when our own planet's shadow illuminates
just how slowly but surely
we ourselves are turning.

Maura

for her thirteenth birthday

In the oven heat of a secret canyon,
we cross the anxious creek to cool.
You reach back to steady me
and your new-sprung strength opens
our eyes. Our footprints, as we
struggle out the other side,
burn off quickly, wet black
into silent white stone.

Mock orange ignites like girl's
perfume, and underneath it
crushed sage in the pinched air
carries me back to my first passion –
your father in high desert.
Away from my valley garden,
I feel your age, the agony
inside your beauty.

Like me, you need something to push
against. We bleed on opposite sides
of the moon. Yours waxing, you
pace with claws and growl while I
calmly plant leaf crops beyond you.
Your lithe hips let the current move
around you, your small breasts ache
inside the long wait. No longer
satisfied in the large yard of my hug.

Now when you come to be held
we rest our heads on the other's shoulder.
How fragile your skull at birth,
two days fighting the tight fist of my cervix.
In your skin, clear from darkness,
I saw blue veins leading to your heart.

That Kiss

Why can one unhurried kiss
arrest us, travel like saxophone sounds
through vocal chord and solar plexus,
enter the spine with ravenous hands
that glide to the inner thigh, caress
us, but another – kiss that abounds –
goes no further than the light-winged
lips of a child, close but without bliss?

Familiar Mystery

Sometimes I catch your boyhood still
playing across your countenance
while you concentrate on something else.
Your lower lip curls out, pushing
the upper lip inward, into your mouth.
Before I ever kissed it open
I memorized that face by heart
and all the lines of daylight since then
have never made illegible
the time before I called you mine.

Lost and Found

My thighs pressed into
your hips,

my calves locked across
your back,

are the only grip I have

when our longing avalanches
and our bodies

find themselves lost inside
the other's.

In the quiet afterward
I wonder

at how seamlessly we stand up
and walk away

fully belonging to our self again.

Rings

Somewhere, I'm sure, in the earth I have tended, I lost the ring
    you slipped
onto my finger twenty three years ago when we had nothing
    to give

but passionate instinct and the naiveté of love's beginnings.
    I know it is there
because I would have felt it slide off in the air, but not when
    my hand was planted

in earth. Since then, it's been replaced with one more expensive,
    tiny diamonds
embedded in it. You, on the other hand, lost yours at the kitchen table,
    when,

in a game where the sound of a ring would have given away
    what is hidden
in the hand, you removed it. For weeks you wandered, feeling
    naked, untruthfully

available in the eyes of the single world, wondering how
it could have vanished in your home. I almost purchased
    you a new one,

but just days before Valentine's Day, it materialized -- rising
    to the surface
and beautifully posed at the top of the mound of coins where
    we empty our pockets

of change each evening. Could it be that your wealth lies
    beneath your promise
to love me and mine is forever planted in the garden
    from which we eat?

Gravity In Our Hands

We forget about the universe,
buried under cloud cover.
Our own lives loom larger
and larger, our heartbeat
settles on the rhythm of others'.

Last night we made our bed
on grass, under stars that fell
and converged as we rolled into one.
The dogs' barks bounced
from boundary line to boundary line
before they circled the sorrowful
howl of the coyotes' feast.
And somewhere, a cougar-story
your grandfather gave us
came alive, prowled around us until
we could feel our hearts' red alert,
could hear our own pulse climbing wildly.

In the morning human sounds,
like sticks and stones, wake us
but we wear something new.
Light, older than earth, slips in
and the darkness we wrapped around
our skin remains to be seen.

When we walk the bright green fields
where leaf and stem are stacked
against winter's hunger and summer
is silently folding itself into
stray piles of rocks, the sun pours over
your hair, the color of dry grass.

Our hands find the others'
gravitational hold and pull
with all the time in the world.

Paul

My son is made from air,
conceived under a piano at noon,

he arrived in absolute peace
without the usual cry

after his first breath.
I held him like loss, afraid

I could ruin him.
When he was three I kissed his stillness

as he slept and he said
through fluttering eyes,

"It does not take so long
to become a man in this world"

and I said, "Yes" softly,
as if there was someone else

in the room … I thought so.
At ten he disappeared on the Continental

Divide, east falling from west,
when for a moment we couldn't keep up.

A strange line of strangers
trudging through snow in tennis shoes

said they had seen him following
mountain goats. Goat Boy!

His room, his choice,
is the deep blue of dawn

(you can't stay in it) or dusk
and filled with tiny accessories,

small plastic men who do good.
At age eleven I catch him

in costume but he freezes,
acts natural and invites

me to sit down while he changes
back into boy again.

His lips are the softest, fullest
that have ever met mine,

he slips his hand into my hand in a crowd.
How did I think about men before him?

His father now cries when he does. His grandmother
cannot see him. In the filtered light

of his sister's shadow he will always be
smaller, never outshine her.

He balances our world
from his deep blue room, with his wall of hats.

The Garden Fence

When you leaned on the fence
and I on my shovel,
where I had been unearthing
the hidden stores of potatoes,
you said you were in love
with light and I thought
you said you were in love
with life and I agreed
that I was too. As we spoke,
every word made sense
for what we thought
the other was saying, each
with our own idea, each
so intricately entwined,
as we are, and when I realized
our mistake I had to laugh
at how, like our conversation
across the fence,
our love works.

The Copper Vase

For Thanksgiving, we steal velvet brown
cattails from the refuge of marsh's solitude,
place them in the copper pitcher you gave me
on my birthday, a gift I will fill.

In summer it held an extravagance of round
faces of sunflowers who somehow continued
to slowly turn their heads, follow the stream
of sunlight as it traveled across the sill.

But now those flowers are black, turned down
over fallow ground, seeds loosed
by the hungry birds in leafless trees
who'll leave before the hard frost's kill.

These cattails describe our season now,
stark in their darkness, remaining true,
refusing to rot, or even to grieve
by growing tougher in night's chill.

In the graceful vase they abound.
Because the stems are dry, there's no use
to add water, so it's a surprise to see
cracks open in the spears, a white spill,

as one by one they fissure and drop clouds:
entire universes of shining parachutes,
each dangling a sliver of gold seed
wishing for spring, for the wind's skill.

Even bare, the vessel form is proud,
forged for beauty, its presence imbues
the room with fire, the eye is pleased.
With your earthy gift my heart is tilled.

Dusk's Ghazal

It's time, open wine fermented in the Red Hill's brimming dreams.
Let's drink from the fruit grown close to us before we swim in dreams.

Half our lives spent together and half of that curled up in sleep,
composing intricate letters to ourselves in spinning dreams.

Thousands of pins spilling down ladders from our mothers' quilts;
each dawn we piece together deeper meanings by skimming dreams.

Remember when we first slept entwined, holding back, platonic?
We woke intimate, knowing we were in love's beginning dreams.

Years have shaped our mysteries into cups that contain the other.
Our faithfulness by day hopes to keep away our sin in dreams.

Still you believe the best of life is yet to be with me, Noël.
May we always be seen and held in silvery winning dreams!

Gleanings

From a beige dream where a shock of red was the heart
of the meaning escaping me, I swim to the shore of dawn;
when did I stop missing the bright stain of blood
that woke me one dawn each month?

Even sheep have routines, waiting for me after first light.
Later they'll walk single-file – white clouds
against an evergreen forest – on the bare trail
they've trodden over all the years here.

Bare branches come back to life – rose and gold – rim
French Prairie. I walk listening to the meanderings
of my companions but secretly I'm memorizing
silence, the edges that will gather in the poem of morning.

White sun in a white sky, and I on my knees in my garden,
where I've tilled in manure it breathes,
even in December. Weeding, I leave
a clear dark path behind me.

Eating the last of the apples
to fall from the tree, I reawaken
desire; the other hunger
hidden inside me.

In the kitchen, a single burgundy lily –
left over from Thanksgiving's bouquet –
holds its own between two candles
and four bowls of kale and potatoes.

Lying in front of the fire as the house grows quiet,
I fall asleep and wake to hot embers, thinking,
if we do have auras, when we love another
they meld to make a third color that becomes us.

About the Author

Noël Hanlon began writing seriously in 1994 when she attended the Flight of the Mind workshop on the McKenzie River in Oregon. Her poems have been published in the US and Ireland. She is a member of a small poetry group which includes several inspirational writers, including Ursula Le Guin and Molly Gloss. She has served on the board of Soapstone, an Oregon residency that provides women writers with a stretch of uninterrupted time for their creative work, and the opportunity to live in semi-solitude in the natural world. Noël herself lives this dream; her own poetry is born out of her relationships with the people, landscapes and animals, tame and wild, of her native Oregon.

Photograph by Maura Koehler-Hanlon